GROUNDHOG DAY

The first little groundhog
crept out of his lair.

(Fingers creep)

The second little groundhog said,
"Is spring in the air?"

(Eyes look up)

The third little groundhog asked,
"Is the time right?"

(Look at wrist
watch)

The fourth little groundhog squirmed,
"The sun is too bright!"

(Cover eyes)

The fifth little groundhog squeaked,
"My shadow I see!"

(Look over
shoulder at
shadow)

"I'm not staying out here!
No, siree! Not ME!"

(Shake head
"No")

"Back to my burrow
I'm going to creep."

(Fingers creep)

"And for six more weeks
I'm going to sleep!"

(Eyes closed;
hands by
face)

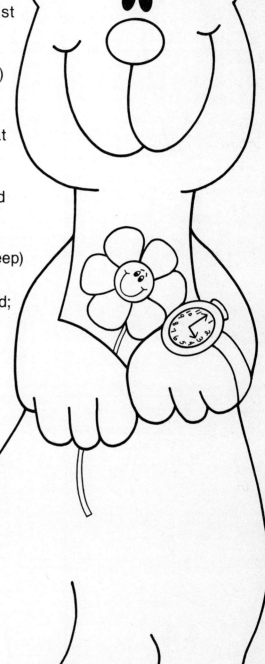

Dear Parent,
    You and your child may wish to share
this poem and its finger movements.
Hope you enjoy it!

© Carson-Dellosa Publ. CD-7003

Color the pictures in each row that are the same.

2

SUNSHINE

1. Color and cut out all of the pieces.
2. Glue the rays to the sun by placing the rays behind the sun.

© Carson-Dellosa Publ. CD-7003

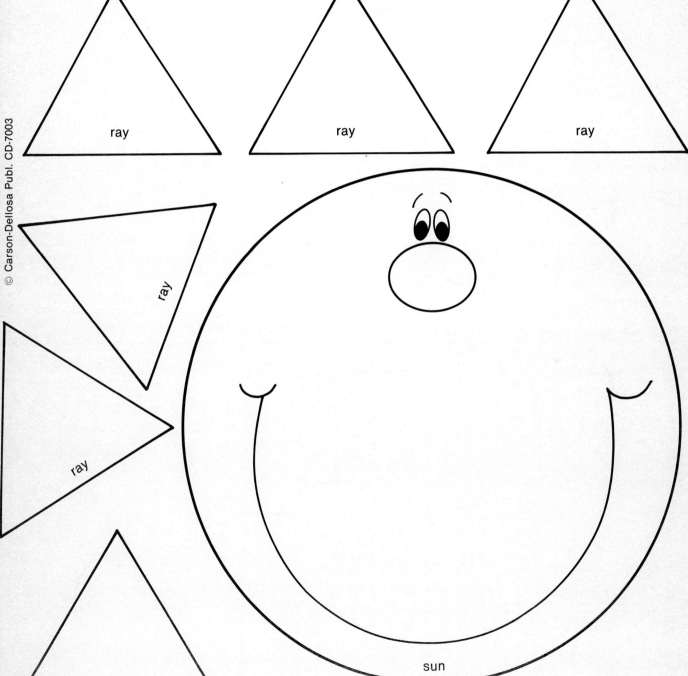

ray

ray

ray

ray

ray

ray

sun

BE MY VALENTINE

We sit down to draw a heart,
       draw a heart, draw a heart,   (Fingers make a heart)
We sit down to draw a heart,
       For Happy Valentine's Day.

We begin to color the heart,
       color the heart, color the heart,   (Fingers color the heart)
We begin to color the heart,
       For Happy Valentine's Day.

Into the mailbox it will go,
       it will go, it will go,   (Heart goes into mailbox)
Into the mailbox it will go,
       For Happy Valentine's Day.

The mailman brings the pretty heart,
       the pretty heart, the pretty heart,   (Child hands heart to next child)
The mailman brings the pretty heart,
       On Happy Valentine's Day.

The pretty heart says "I love you,
       I love you, I love you,"   (Finger points to self;
The pretty heart says, "I love you,"   finger points to next child)
       On Happy Valentine's Day.

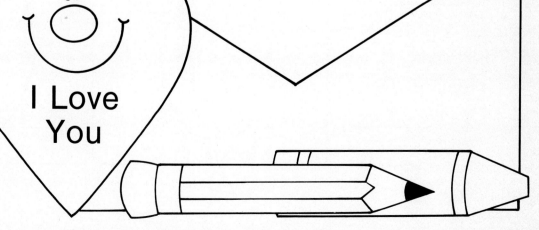

Dear Parent,
  You and your child may wish to share this poem and its finger movements. Hope you enjoy it!

Please Be Mine

I Love You

Color the pictures in each row that are the same.

5

HAPPY HEART

1. Color and cut out all of the pieces.
2. Glue the triangles to the circle by placing the triangles behind the circle to form a bow. (See example.)
3. Glue the bow to the bottom of the heart.
4. Draw a face on the heart.

triangle

triangle

heart

circle

(Pull-Out Poster)

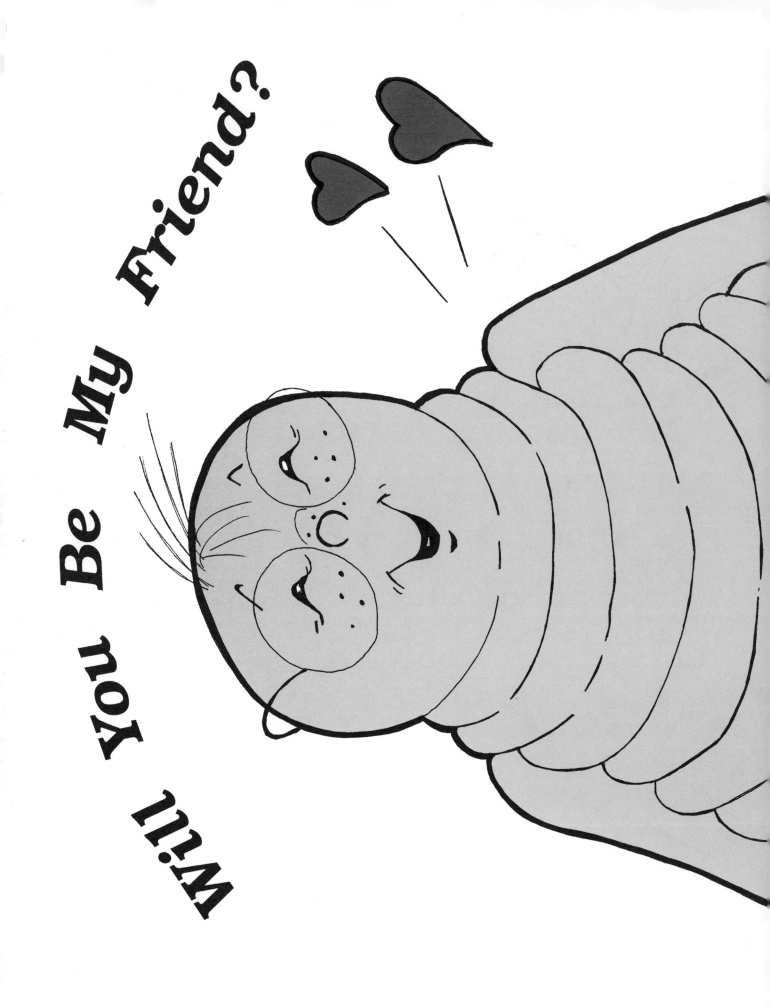

Please Take Good Care of Books!

*(Pull-Out
Poster)*

GEORGE WASHINGTON

George's little ax goes up.
(All fingers go up)

George's little ax goes down.
(All fingers go down)

George's little cherry tree
(Fingertips together to
form a "tree")

Falls down to the ground.
(Fingers and hands
flutter down)

Dear Parent,
    You and your child may wish to share this poem and its finger movements. Hope you enjoy it!

© Carson-Dellosa Publ. CD-7003

7

Color the pictures in each row that are the same.

8

WASHINGTON'S AX

1. Color and cut out all of the pieces.
2. Glue the blade to the top of the handle. (See example.)

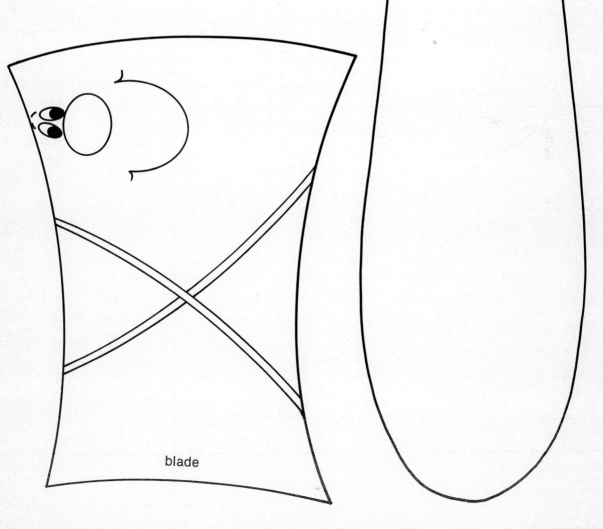

blade

handle

FIVE IRISH SHAMROCKS

Five little shamrocks hopping through the door,
  (Five fingers hop)
One chased a tiny elf, and then there were four.
  (Hold up 4 fingers)

Four little shamrocks swinging in a tree,
  (Fingers swing)
One tumbled down, and then there were three.
  (Hold up 3 fingers)

Three little shamrocks heard an owl say "WHOO!"
  (Fingers at ears)
One hid behind a leprechaun, and then there were two.
  (Hold up 2 fingers)

Two little shamrocks said, "Let's do a little dance."
  (Fingers dance)
One soon tired out, one was left to prance.
  (Hold up 1 finger)

One little shamrock left, left all alone to say,
  (Hands cup mouth)
"I'm going to do a little jig. Happy St. Patrick's Day!"
  (Finger does a jig)

Dear Parent,
  You and your child may wish to share this poem and its finger movements. Hope you enjoy it!

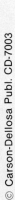

Color the pictures in each row that are the same.

11

SHAMROCK

1. Color and cut out all of the pieces.
2. Glue one leaf to each side of the stem.
   (See example.)

stem

leaf

leaf

FIVE BABY BUNNIES

Five baby bunnies hopping out to play,
Hopping in the forest on happy Easter Day.
 (Fingers hopping)

The first baby bunny carried his new cane,
He twirled it as he came hopping down the lane.
 (Twirl cane in the air)

The second baby bunny came to the river's brink,
Tasted the cool water and took a long, long drink.
 (Stoop down, take drink)

The third baby bunny tied her bonnet so new,
Under her chin, a bow of pink, white and blue.
 (Tie bow under chin)

The fourth baby bunny skipped down the shady lane,
He opened his umbrella just in case of rain.
 (Open umbrella)

The fifth baby bunny said, "Look what I see!"
Lots and lots of colored eggs hiding near the tree!"
 (Eyes cupped)

Dear Parent,
 You and your child may wish to share this poem and its finger movements. Hope you enjoy it!

Color the pictures in each row that are the same.

14

EASTER BUNNY

1. Color and cut out all of the pieces.
2. Glue the nose to the center of the head.
3. Glue the eyes to the head by placing the eyes above the nose.
4. Glue the ears to the head by placing the ears behind the top of the head. (See example.)
5. Draw a mouth.

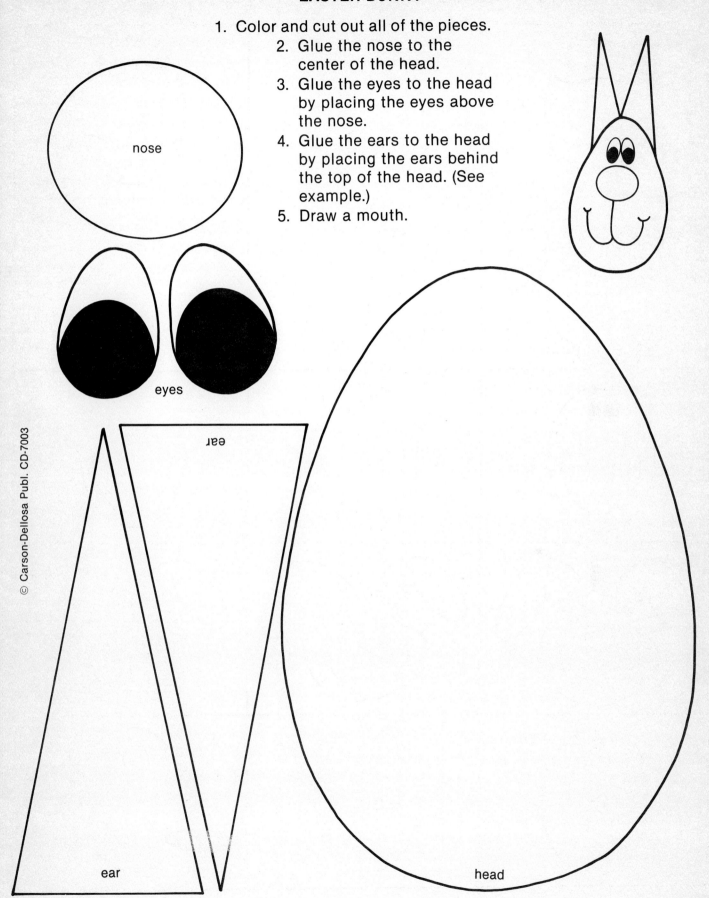

nose

eyes

ear

ear

head

FIVE LITTLE GHOSTS

Five little ghosts were swinging on a gate.
    (Fingers swing)

The first little ghost said, "I think it's almost eight." (Look at wrist)

The second little ghost said, "I'm going out to howl." (Hands around mouth)

The third little ghost said, "I'm going out to prowl." (Hands around eyes)

The fourth little ghost said, "The moon is far too bright." (Eyes covered)

The fifth little ghost said, "Let's FLY . .it's Halloween night!" (Fingers fly)

Dear Parent,
    You and your child may wish to share this poem and its finger movements. Hope you enjoy it!

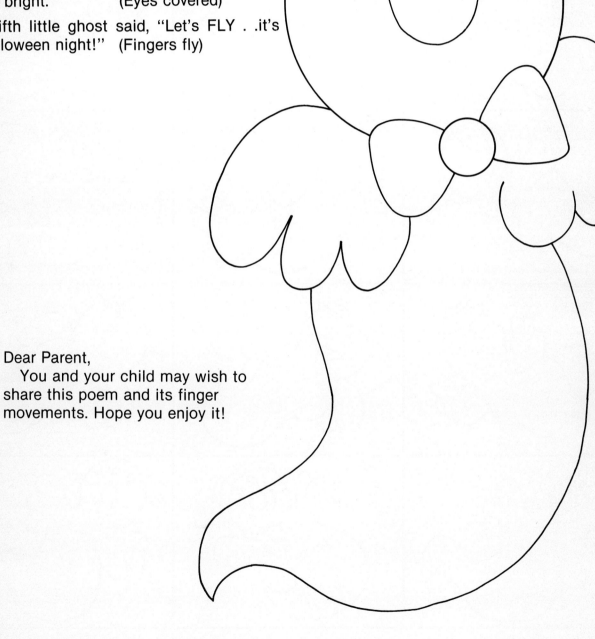

Color the pictures in each row that are the same.

17

GHOST

1. Color and cut out all of the pieces.
2. Glue the bow to the middle of the ghost. (See example.)
3. Glue the eyes to the ghost by placing the eyes near the top of the ghost's head. (See example.)
4. Glue the nose to the ghost by placing the nose below the eyes.
5. Draw a mouth.

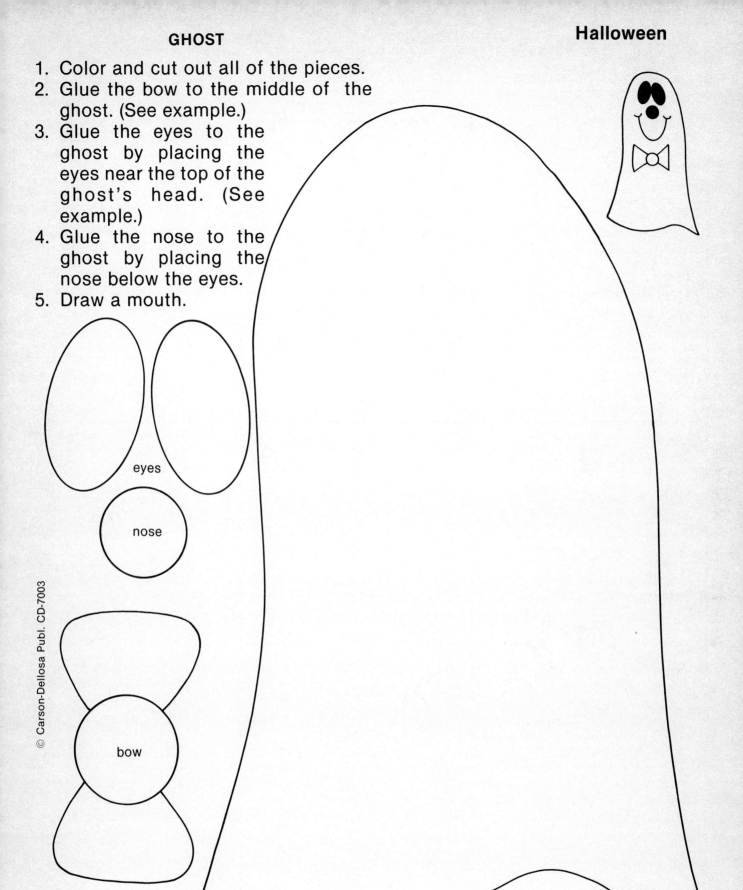

eyes

nose

bow

ghost body

© Carson-Dellosa Publ. CD-7003

SIX LITTLE INDIANS

Six little Indians said, "Let's stop our games and play."
                    (Six moving fingers stop)

"We'll walk to join the Pilgrims for their
    Thanksgiving Day."   (Fingers walk away)

They joined them at the table, and placed their hands
   to pray.   (Fingers in prayer position)

The Indians bowed their heads and blessed
   Thanksgiving Day.   (Children bow their heads)

Dear Parent,
   You and your child may wish to share
this poem and its finger movements.
Hope you enjoy it!

Color the pictures in each row that are the same.

20

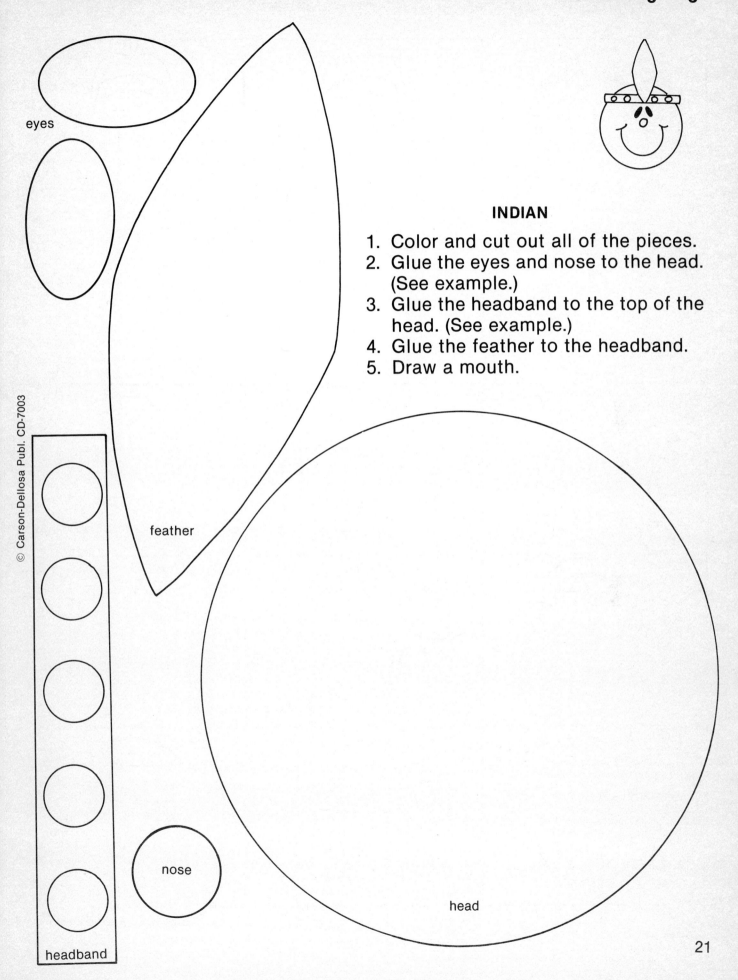

eyes

© Carson-Dellosa Publ. CD-7003

INDIAN

1. Color and cut out all of the pieces.
2. Glue the eyes and nose to the head. (See example.)
3. Glue the headband to the top of the head. (See example.)
4. Glue the feather to the headband.
5. Draw a mouth.

feather

nose

head

headband

SANTA'S REINDEERS

Eight little reindeer in Santa's toy heaven,	(Hold up 8 fingers)
Dasher fell asleep, and then there were seven.	(Hands by face sleeping)
Seven little reindeer, with bags full of tricks,	(Carrying bags over shoulder)
Dancer stubbed his toe, and then there were six.	(Stub toe, hold up 6 fingers)
Six little reindeer, all wanted to drive,	(Holding wheel)
Prancer became cold, and then there were five.	(Hold up five fingers)
Five little reindeer said, "Let's eat once more."	(Fingers to mouth)
Vixen got a tummyache, and then there were four.	(Rub stomach; hold up 4 fingers)
Four little reindeer looking out at sea,	(Hands over eyes)
Comet jumped in, and then there were three.	(Fingers jump; hold up 3 fingers)
Three little reindeer, wearing bells so new,	(Hands on head)
Cupid took his off, and then there were two.	(Take bell off; hold up 2 fingers)
Two little reindeer said, "We're going to run."	(Two fingers run)
Donder did a somersault, and then there was one.	(Finger somersaults; 1 finger up)
One little reindeer, left to pull Santa's sleigh,	(Hands hold reins)
Blitzen called out, "Merry Christmas! Have a good day!"	(Fingers cup mouth)

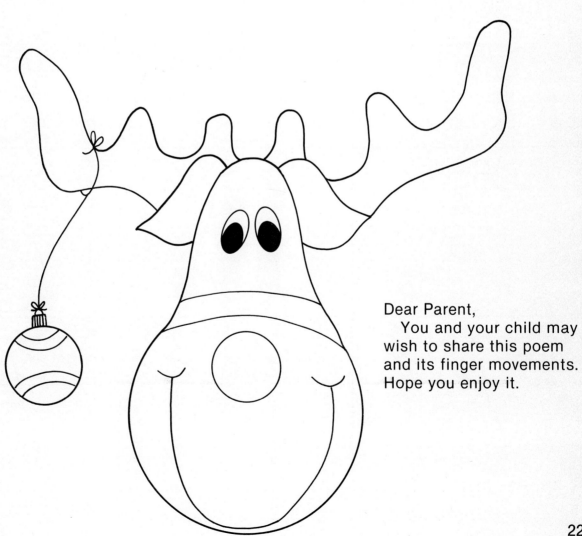

Dear Parent,
  You and your child may wish to share this poem and its finger movements. Hope you enjoy it.

Color the pictures in each row that are the same.

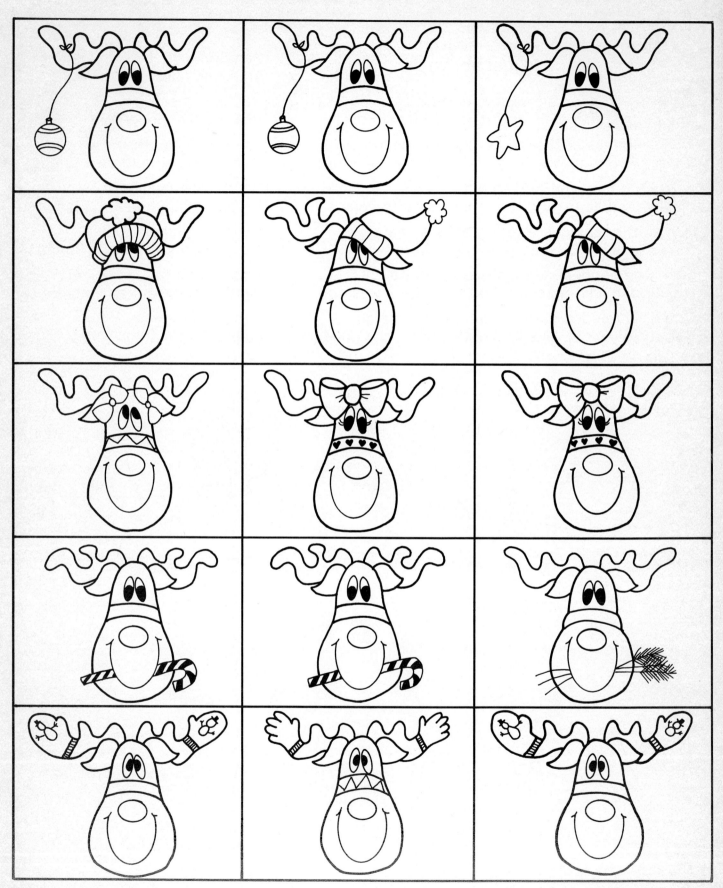

23

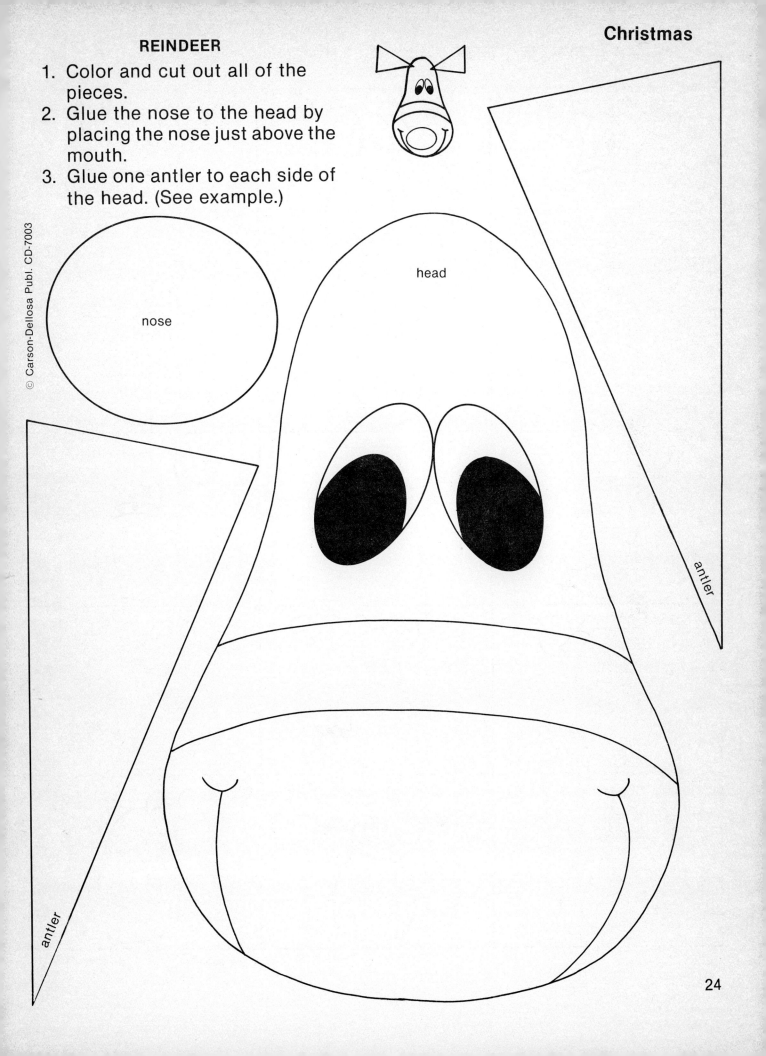

REINDEER

1. Color and cut out all of the pieces.
2. Glue the nose to the head by placing the nose just above the mouth.
3. Glue one antler to each side of the head. (See example.)

nose

head

antler

antler

24